# Sow and Grow Rich

# SOW & GROW RICH

## Dr. Leroy Thompson Sr.

Ever Increasing Word Ministries
Darrow, LA

Unless otherwise indicated, all scripture quotations are taken from the *King James Version* of the Bible. Direct quotations from the Bible appear italicized or bolded.

*Sow and Grow Rich.*

Paperback ISBN-13: 978-0-9632584-6-5

e-book ISBN-13: 978-0-9632584-9-6

Copyright © 2019 by Dr. Leroy Thompson Sr.

Published by: *Ever Increasing Word Ministries.*
P.O. Box 7
Darrow, LA 70725

Author websites: leroythompson.tv, eiwm.org

Printed in the United States of America. All rights reserved under International Copyright Law. Contents and/or cover may not be reproduced in whole or in part in any form without the express written consent of the Publisher.

# Contents

| | |
|---|---|
| Before we begin... | 1 |
| **Ch. 1** Why Sow? | 5 |
| **Ch. 2** A Principle of the Kingdom | 11 |
| **Ch. 3** Seedtime and Harvest | 17 |
| **Ch. 4** Faith and a Seed | 25 |
| **Ch. 5** God Watches Over His Seed | 29 |
| **Ch. 6** Activate Heaven's Supply | 35 |
| **Ch. 7** Sowing Grace | 41 |
| **Ch. 8** Catch The Seed Blocker | 49 |
| **Ch. 9** Take the Weights Off | 55 |
| **Ch. 10** The Seed Always Prevails | 61 |
| **Ch. 11** Be a Seed Pusher | 69 |
| **Ch. 12** Be Adventurous | 75 |
| **Ch. 13** Manifest From Within | 83 |
| Keep this in your heart. | 95 |
| About the Author | 97 |

# Before we begin...

*Are you teachable?* That's the first question I have for you. Teaching comes with change.

The second question is: *What type of financial system do you have set up in your life that's not working?* Whatever it is, let's cut it down.

There are some things you've been carrying and have learned over the years that haven't been working as it should, but it's time for that tree to come down. If you've been doing the same thing and nothing has changed, cut it down. I'm here to help you do it.

Isaiah 48:17 says, "Thus saith the Lord, thy Redeemer, the Holy One of Israel; I am the Lord thy God which teacheth thee to profit, which leadeth thee by the way that thou shouldest go." Notice it says "teacheth thee to profit" and not teacheth thee to fail or teacheth thee to stay at the same level. This means you can be taught how to profit.

But again, are you teachable?

I'm teaching you how to sow and grow rich. That's the way I did it. I'm rich because I sowed. I followed the Bible's way to prosperity. Many people tried to talk me out of it. They said I was giving my money away, but really I was sowing my money, not giving anything away. I had expectation. Then, I had visitation. Then, I had manifestation. Then, I had demonstration. Then, I had creation. I'm looking for you to have the same things in your life. I'm writing this so that my grace and anointing to sow and grow rich will be on you.

---

**SAY THIS ALOUD**

*Holy Spirit, develop a pure desire in me to sow.*

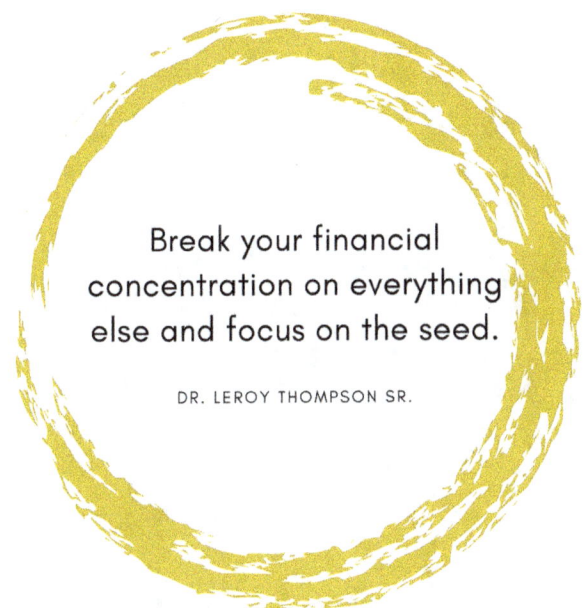

Break your financial concentration on everything else and focus on the seed.

DR. LEROY THOMPSON SR.

# 1.

# Why Sow?

Sowing is a blessing from God to make you rich. It's a divine way to prosperity that Satan has tried to turn into something else. For years, force and fear have been involved with giving in the Church. It is sad that the majority of churchgoers can say they've experienced ministers saying almost anything in the pulpit to pressure them to give. That shouldn't be! Giving should be about faith and cooperation, not fear and force. When people are taught properly and recognize that sowing is what they are supposed to do to grow, no one will have to twist their arms to do it.

Sowing aims to take you to another level and into a greater dimension of walking in the blessings of God. We see this in Genesis 12. God taught Abraham the principles of sowing and trained him to be a sower. The first verse of Genesis 12 says:

**Now the Lord said unto Abram, <u>Get thee out of thy country, and from thy kindred, and from thy father's house</u>, unto a land that I will shew thee**.

**Genesis 12:1**

That's the beginning of Abraham's training. We'll go deeper into what happens after this step, but first understand this: To be a bonafide sower, you will have to leave some things and some people behind.

Notice, the Lord also added where Abraham would be going. He said, "unto a land that I will show you." What type of land is God talking about? If we look at Deuteronomy 8:7-10, it tells us.

**[7] For the Lord thy God bringeth <u>thee into a good land</u>, a land of brooks of water, of fountains and depths that spring out of valleys and hills; [8] A land of wheat, and barley, and vines, and fig trees, and pomegranates; a land of oil olive, and honey; [9] A land wherein thou shalt eat bread <u>without scarceness</u>, thou shalt not lack anything in it; a land whose stones are iron, and out of whose hills thou mayest dig**

**brass. [10] When thou hast eaten and art full, then thou shalt bless the Lord thy God for the good land which he hath given thee.**
**Deuteronomy 8:7-10**

There are three types of lands you can go into:

- The land of not enough
- The land of just enough
- The land of more than enough

Sowing will take you into the land of more than enough — a *good* land, a land of harvest, without scarcity, flowing with milk and honey. You should be living in the land of more than enough. You should never lack anything you want or anything you desire, dream, or see. Too many Christians are living in lack and scarceness. But that's not of God — that's of religion and tradition.

If we look back at Genesis 12, going into the next two verses, we see a demonstration of sowing. It states:

**[2] And I will make of thee a great nation, and I will bless thee, and make thy name great;**

**[3] And thou shalt be a blessing: and I will bless them that bless thee, and curse him that curseth thee: and in thee shall all the families of the earth be blessed.**

**Genesis 12:2-3**

God said, "I'll bless them that bless you." That's a demonstration of sowing. He was telling Abraham, "Teach them to sow like I'm teaching you to do, and when they sow into you, I'll sow into them."

The type of blessings you see in Abraham's life couldn't have happened without sowing. In Genesis 13:2, it says: **Abram was very rich in cattle, in silver, and in gold**. Again, this cannot happen without sowing. Why? Because God would have to shipwreck His entire system. If Abraham wasn't a sower, a lot of other things God tells us in His Word would be a lie. And we know God is not a man that He should lie. If He said it, He'll make it good (Numbers 23:19).

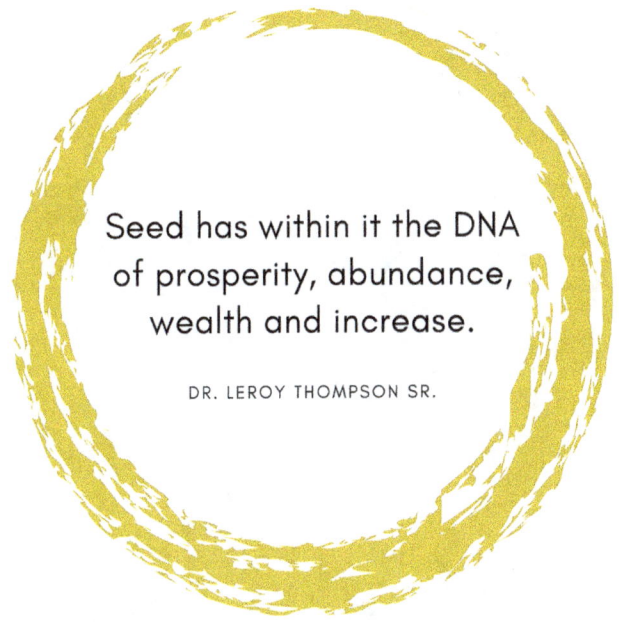

Seed has within it the DNA of prosperity, abundance, wealth and increase.

DR. LEROY THOMPSON SR.

# 2.

# A Principle of the Kingdom

There's a heavenly system set up to bless you, but don't think you're so special that you're going to walk into a dimension of more than enough without sowing. The kingdom of God is a seed kingdom (meaning it operates by seed), and it's set up to function in your favor. In Matthew 6:33, Jesus says: **But seek ye first the kingdom of God, and his righteousness; and all these things shall be added unto you**. The key revelation here is that "seeking the kingdom" is also about seeking *how* the kingdom functions and seeking *what* makes the kingdom operate. I'm telling you now that the seed is the how and what behind the way the kingdom operates. God does nothing without a seed. God Himself is a sower!

**For God so loved the world, that he gave His only begotten Son, that whosoever believeth in**

**Him should not perish, but have everlasting life.**

**John 3:16**

God wanted a family, so He sowed a seed to reap one. If you notice, the conversation about the seed didn't start with prosperity teachers. It started long ago as a principle of the kingdom of God.

Once God taught the sowing system to Abraham, Abraham taught his son Isaac. We see Isaac in action in Genesis 26, and we learn a great lesson from him.

**Then Isaac sowed in that land** [a land of famine]**, and received in the same year an hundredfold: and the LORD blessed him.**

**Genesis 26:12**

Isaac sowed in famine and received a hundredfold. What does this mean for you? It means that regardless of the condition you are in today, you can sow and receive a harvest, even a return of a hundred times as much. There is absolutely no condition a seed can't change. In the same way, there is no bill a seed can't pay. If you pay attention to what is said in this book, the Holy Spirit will be able to take you somewhere greater with a seed.

The way you overcome the enemy in your finances is by a seed. The way you overcome generational curses and how your ancestors lived is by sowing your way out of the level they lived on. No one in my family lives like me. The seed changed my life so much that some of my family members don't even recognize me. Just like that, the seed is ready to change *your* life and take you to another level.

If you watch the lives of people who consistently give, you'll notice that after a while their lives elevate to another level. They go to a higher place in their giving and their lifestyle. For instance, I remember a time when my wife and I went on a cruise with a friend of ours who knew a little more about how things functioned on the ship. As the speaker welcomed everyone aboard and went over logistics, our friend turned to us and said, "Look at the people on this first floor real good because you're not going to see them anymore."

I had no idea what he was talking about until after the orientation ended and another lady walked up. Holding a clipboard, she started calling out names — our names were included. She led the few of us who were called upstairs to an entirely new spectrum of living, and exactly as our friend said, the majority of the people stayed downstairs. We didn't see them anymore. On the higher level of that ship, we enjoyed better service. It felt like another world up there. I'm telling you this to show you where you're headed. That's where the seed is ready to take you. You're headed off the bottom floor of your finances.

Sow, because it's a principle of the kingdom set up to take you to another level — a level off of this world's system. There's another place for the righteous to live. We have to let our light shine in our finances from this day forward.

I'd like for you to travel deeper with me through the Word of God that proves you are destined to sow and grow rich, just as Abraham did — just as I did.

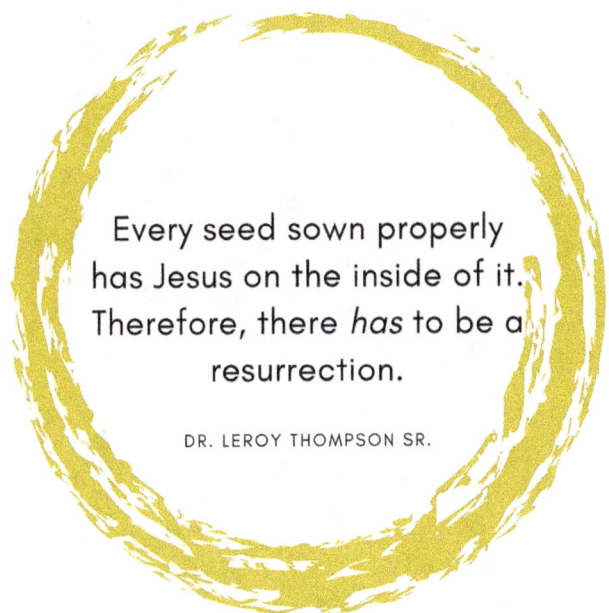

Every seed sown properly has Jesus on the inside of it. Therefore, there *has* to be a resurrection.

DR. LEROY THOMPSON SR.

# 3.

# Seedtime and Harvest

**While the earth remaineth, <u>seedtime and harvest</u>, and cold and heat, and summer and winter, and day and night shall not cease.**

**Genesis 8:22**

*Seedtime and harvest... shall not cease.* Seedtime and harvest is God's divine plan to free you and take you off of the plans and systems of man. Many have become familiar with the phrase "seedtime and harvest" and fail to see that it's impregnating. The harvest grows out of the seed, and the seed grows out of the harvest. There is no such thing as seedtime without harvest, and there is no such thing as harvest without the seed. It's a principle that won't cease. The whole spectrum of the kingdom of God manifestation is hidden in the mystery of the seed. Prosperity, wealth, increase, and abundance is hidden in the mystery of the seed, and as a child of God, that mystery is available to you.

In Matthew 13:11-12, Jesus, the Master Seed Trainer, says: **It is given unto you to know the mystery of the kingdom of heaven. For whosoever hath, to him shall be given, and he shall have more abundance: but whosoever hath not, from him shall be taken away even that he hath**. Here, Jesus was teaching a masterful lesson on how the kingdom functions. It's given to you to know the mystery of the kingdom, and the key mystery of the kingdom is knowing the operation, function, and production of the seed. It's very simple. It means that your debt cancellation, your good life, and everything you want to produce financially in your life is yours through the understanding and realization of the seed. Again, it's given to you to know the mystery of the kingdom, and the mystery of the kingdom is the seed.

So, how have you been trying to get free financially? By a salary or by a seed? I'm not teaching you about what you can earn from a college education or a good salary. I'm talking about kingdom education and kingdom income. Unlike the world's system, no one can say they are left out of God's system of seedtime and harvest. If you don't get into college or finish school, you can be left out of the world's system of a good education and a good salary, but you can't be left out of this! Regardless of your condition or intellect, it's set up to bless you. If you are a child of God, you can do this! You don't have to have a high IQ to know that God has put something in your hand and you can sow it.

You may think because you don't see a seed in your pocket right now that you can't do this, but you're mistaken. In Second Corinthians 9:10, we see there is no excuse for not having a seed. It says: **Now <u>he that ministereth seed to the sower</u> both minister bread for your food, and multiply your seed sown, and increase the fruits of your righteousness**. He that ministereth seed to the sower — not to the crook. God gives seed to *the sower*. Not to the one who will spend it and act as if He is not doing what He said He'd do. Many times, God has given you seed but you bought something with it.

Listen, you're not going to become prosperous if you keep eating (or spending) the seed God gave you to sow. You have to sow until you sweat

— until you almost come into regret. The kingdom of God is a seed kingdom, not a "saying" kingdom. Confession can't take the place of sowing. You have to do more than talk about it. You have to actually use your hands to sow. Sowing can even hurt sometimes, but as you keep doing it, it gets easier. Sow your way out of the natural and into the supernatural financial plan of God.

Yes, God has a supernatural financial plan for you called sowing. (*It's not called a job. It's called sowing.*) If you are ever going to reach where God wants you to be financially and live prosperously, you will have to understand that the supernatural financial plan for you is not prayer. In saying that, I'm not taking anything away from the power of prayer, but the supernatural plan for your *finances* is sowing. Due to the lack of understanding in the Church, we've tried to pray everything down from heaven, but what most fail to realize is that most things are already down here.

We pray, praise, dance, shout, sing, and worship, but it all comes down to the point of sowing in this area. This is very important to understand. Sowing doesn't take a second place to praising and praying, but it is the key to the operation and functioning of the kingdom that the enemy can't understand nor stop.

I've had people try to stop me, but they couldn't do it. I continued, year after year, to function in the spiritual law of seedtime and harvest. I also functioned in another spiritual law that goes along with seedtime and harvest — love.

Love never fails (1 Corinthians 13:8). So, when you sow, sow in love. Never allow the people who get upset when you sow to offend you. Keep on sowing. Seedtime and harvest will keep you balanced and operating in the love of God. When you sow and grow rich, it's never about going after money. It's about consistently working the principles God has in place. The principles will cause money to come after *you*.

My life is evidence that the principle of seedtime and harvest works! I came from nothing, and now I don't even have to pray for or think about money anymore. I just do what God tells me to do and it comes. Prayer isn't made for money. The seed is made for money. This is why the Church has been stuck on the same level and in the same condition for so long. They've been praying about money. Yelling, "I need this" or "I need that." While, on the other hand, God is steadily saying: "No, I told you the way to do it. I'm going to give you the seed, but I can't sow it for you. I don't do anything without your faith and seed. You have to sow it, and *then*, I can change your condition."

When you sow with understanding, wisdom, and revelation, your faith starts dancing because results are about to hit your life.

DR. LEROY THOMPSON SR.

## 4.

# Faith and a Seed

**And the apostles said unto the Lord, Increase our faith. And the Lord said, <u>If ye had faith as a grain of mustard seed</u>, ye might say unto this sycamine tree, Be thou plucked up by the root, and be thou planted in the sea; and it should obey you.**

**Luke 17:5-6**

It's not an increase in faith you need. All you need is the seed principle and to understand how it works. The seed has authority over plenty, but it's up to you to catch the revelation. Therefore, study the seed. Your faith is already working. You don't need *more* faith. As Jesus explained in Luke 17, even if it's as small as a grain of mustard seed, an entire tree can obey you and be uprooted.

Now, what about your debt and lack? Will it take

*more* faith to uproot it and make it move as you want? No, it won't. In the same way, if your faith is as small as a grain of mustard seed, it'll move. It's not about increasing your faith to get out of debt and lack. It's about your faith needing a seed sown to participate in kingdom finances. Faith without a seed won't work.

Without first having faith and a seed come together, your harvest can't become pregnant with manifestation. Faith can't be impregnated without a seed, and a seed can't be impregnated without faith. Faith must work in the womb of a seed to impregnate it with the manifestations of the promises of God. It's financial intercourse, and it cannot take place without the companionship of faith and a seed.

Think about that.

Your seed has a womb, and when you sow in faith, babies (dreams and manifestations) are born.

> You don't have to be anxious about being taken care of. Only attend to the ministry of sowing.
>
> DR. LEROY THOMPSON SR.

# 5.

# God Watches Over His Seed

**Then said the Lord unto me, Thou hast well seen: for I will hasten my word to perform it.**
**Jeremiah 1:12**

The Word of God and the seed are synonymous. When God said "**I will hasten** [meaning *watch*] **my word to perform it**" in Jeremiah 1:12, He's also saying He will watch over His *seed* to perform it. It's important for your heart, soul, and inner being to hear, trust, and understand that when you sow a seed you're sowing the Word and God is watching over it.

A financial seed sown is full of mercy, grace, righteousness, and understanding because God told you to do it. You're not planting empty money when God's hand is on it. All the promises of God are yea and amen (2 Corinthians 1:20). God is saying, "I promise if you sow, I'll see to it that you have a harvest. You'll never have to want for anything anymore." If you're expecting something and it doesn't show up tomorrow, don't panic. As a bonafide sower with God watching over your seed to perform it, richness cannot escape you.

**[10] For as the rain cometh down, and the snow from heaven, and returneth not thither, but watereth the earth, and maketh it bring forth and bud, that it may give seed to the sower, and bread to the eater: [11] So shall my word be that goeth forth out of my mouth: it shall not return unto me void, but it shall accomplish that which I please, and it shall prosper in the thing whereto I sent it.**

**Isaiah 55:10-11**

You may be thinking: *I'm alone. I'm single. I'm a widow. My job situation isn't too good.* Or, *I have to get my children some things, first.* But do you remember what we learned (in Chapter 1) from Isaac's example of sowing in famine land? Seed sowing does not respect the type of condition you're in or how long you've been in it. It's designed to supernaturally change your condition to produce in your favor. Despite where you may live, the enemy cannot stop you. Understand that *no one* can stop a sower — not the government, economy, politicians, haters, naysayers, religious folks, or denominations. They tried to shut me down from every angle, but they couldn't. I kept sowing.

One of the main things that will rob a seed is the lack of understanding (*which I'm clearing up in this book*). You must have an understanding of the pivotal power of a seed and how precious it is. My wife and I can both attest to the fact that if you want to sow (despite your condition), God will always give you a seed — a seed full of mercy, grace, and righteousness.

Once God gives you seed, you're going to have to sow... and sow and sow! As you break through the sowing flow, the seed keeps on coming. You just have to get in there and start. I'll say this again: *seed sowing does not respect the condition you're in*! Have you truly realized that? Take ahold of this revelation in your heart. No matter where you are right now, God has you here for a reason. No matter what your financial condition is and no matter how long it has been that way, by the revelation of this impartation and the anointing on your life as you read, you're set up for a change of condition. Of course, you can't sow what you don't have, but you can't have what you don't sow.

God will never permit a seed sower to be mocked in their finances. As it says in Galatians 6:7, **God is not mocked**. Well, the seed is of God, so just as God is not mocked, the seed is not mocked. God will not permit you to keep sowing and not manifest. Due season *has* to come. If we keep reading through to Galatians 6:9, it says: **And let us not be weary <u>in well doing</u>: for in <u>due season</u> we shall reap, if we faint not**. Don't faint. Sowing is the *well-doing* we see in that verse. Let us not be weary in sowing. Due season *has* to come.

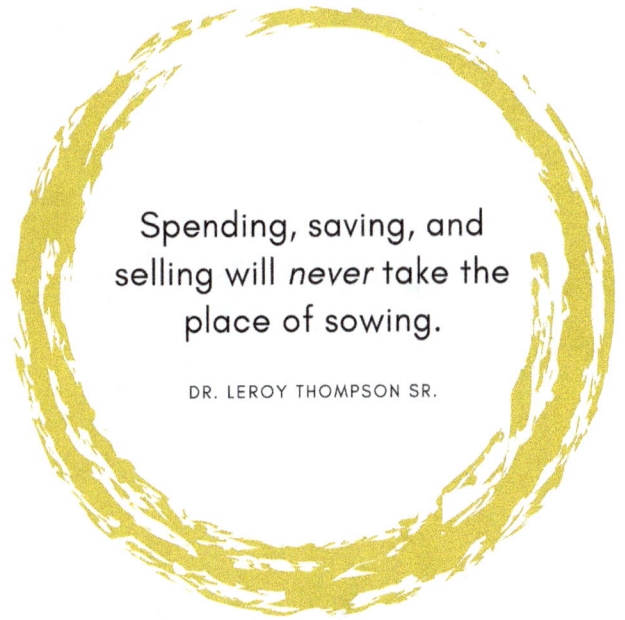

Spending, saving, and selling will *never* take the place of sowing.

DR. LEROY THOMPSON SR.

# 6.

# Activate Heaven's Supply

The seed activates heaven's supply. Now, what kind of supply do you think heaven has? It's limitless. If you want to activate heaven's supply, you're going to have to sow the seed, and when you do, you'll open an account with divine interest.

Your savings account is no match for sowing. There is no institution that will pay interest like God. There are times God comes off the hook with His giving, and you can't keep up with it. I'm a witness. So, if you're sowing, don't give up. Don't become discouraged about whether God wants you blessed. He absolutely does! You may have a lot of religious people and churchgoers pushing against you but keep pressing. Sometimes, you may even have to cry while sowing. Why? Because you're going to want to buy something and the seed is going to scream out, "I'm not for that! Sow me!"

You see, the seed is not prosperous if it's not planted.

> **In the morning sow thy seed, and in the evening withhold not thine hand: for thou knowest not whether shall prosper, either this or that, or whether they both shall be alike good.**
>
> **Ecclesiastes 11:6**

Over the years, I've learned that one seed is not going to get heaven's supply activated in your life. Four or ten seeds aren't going to get it either. You have to become a systematic sower, as we see demonstrated in Ecclesiastes 11:6. Be consistent, not out of pressure but because God told you to do it. Never allow a man to talk money out of your pocket. As I mentioned in Chapter 1, it's not about giving under pressure. Giving should be about faith and cooperation, not fear and force.

The language of a seed says, "God is my source." Therefore, I'm not writing this book because I desire a gift. I desire that fruit may abound in your divine supply account. Since I've started ministering this message on prosperity, I've been trying to help the Body of Christ open their unlimited supply account and learn how to operate with sowing consciousness.

What happens when the Holy Spirit ignites a sowing consciousness in you on purpose? Psalm 126 happens.

**[1] When the Lord turned again the captivity of Zion, we were like them that dream. [2] Then was <u>our mouth filled with laughter</u>, and <u>our tongue with singing</u>: then said they among the heathen, The Lord hath done great things for them. [3] <u>The Lord hath done great things for us</u>; whereof <u>we are glad</u>. [4] Turn again our captivity, O Lord, as the streams in the south. [5] They that sow in tears shall <u>reap in joy</u>. [6] He that goeth forth and weepeth, bearing precious seed, shall doubtless <u>come again with rejoicing</u>, bringing his sheaves with him.**

**Psalm 126: 1-6**

This is what you're being brought into — a life of prosperity with a sowing consciousness. Functioning with a sowing consciousness means being able to see and stop anything in your soul (*which includes anything in your mind, consciousness, imagination, will, reasoning, and emotions*) that has been blocking you from sowing. Besides your own thinking, nothing and no one can stop you from coming into your wealthy place.

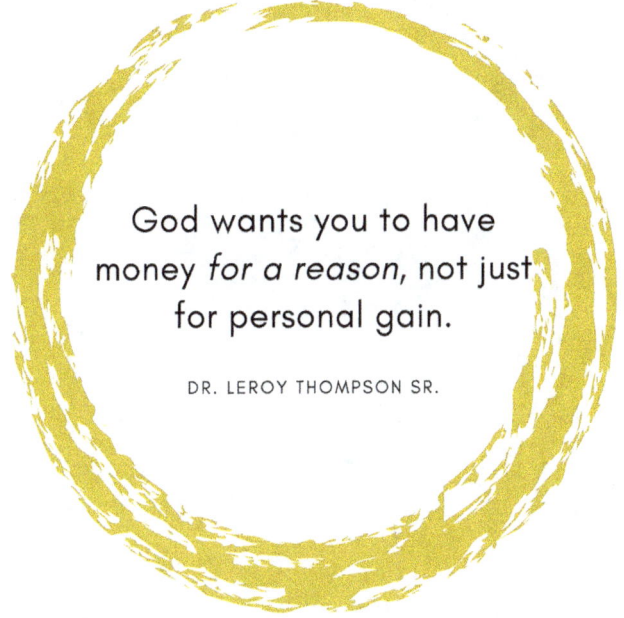

God wants you to have money *for a reason*, not just for personal gain.

DR. LEROY THOMPSON SR.

# 7.

# Sowing Grace

The truth is that you're not going to sow automatically. God can develop a sowing heart in you and give you strong hands to sow, but you will need a grace to *do* it. You have to allow the Holy Spirit to grace you to sow. It is possible that you haven't fully stepped into that aspect of grace yet, and that's what has been holding back your finances. Maybe not being graced to give is why God hasn't trusted you with much. You *must* have a sowing grace on your life to walk in financial freedom.

Read how Paul gives the church of Corinth an example of the Macedonian churches' sowing grace.

**[1] Moreover, brethren, we do you to wit of the grace of God bestowed on the churches of Macedonia;** (*Notice the condition of the church in the next verse.*) **[2] How that in a great trial of**

**affliction the abundance of their joy and their deep poverty abounded unto the riches of their liberality.**

**2 Corinthians 8:1-2**

At the end of the second verse above, we can see the Macedonian churches became liberal when they were broke. In verse 3, Paul goes on to say:

**For to their power, I bear record, yea, and <u>beyond their power</u> they were willing of themselves;**

**2 Corinthians 8:3**

**Beyond their power** means beyond their ability. This is an example for you, too. Ask God to grace you to sow beyond *your* ability. *Your* ability brings *your* results, but God's ability brings godly results. If you never step out beyond your own ability, you'll never see God's results in your life. You have to align your soul ("your thinking, believing, imagining, feeling, consciousness") with God's ability, and that has to be done with a sowing grace.

Have you ever had money afflictions in your life? I'm sure that you have. I've had great trials, *and* I've also had great money. But some of my greatest trials were financial trials, and I sowed through it. So, yes, you'll need to maintain this sowing grace to consistently sow the same way, through the trials and all.

Paul had a revelation from the Holy Spirit in Second Corinthians 9. His point was that sowing has to be done on purpose. In Second Corinthians 9:6-7, it reads:

**[6] But this I say, He which soweth sparingly shall reap also sparingly; and he which soweth bountifully shall reap also bountifully. [7] Every man according as he purposeth in his heart, so let him give; not grudgingly, or of necessity: for God loveth a cheerful giver.**

**2 Corinthians 9:6-7**

You have to sow willingly. You can't sow grudgingly or be forced to sow. Sowing is not a fall; it's a flow. You enter a flow of grace that enables you to trust God and sow by faith. Let me repeat that: *You sow by faith*.

In order to sow willingly, your heart has to be stitched with a sowing grace. Then, you won't be afraid of how your condition looks or how the world's economy looks. It'll no longer matter to you because you'll be operating from another perspective in your finances. You'll be cheerful! But you can't be a cheerful giver without grace.

Let's read further into what Paul said in Second Corinthians 9:8-10.

**[8] And God is able to make all grace abound toward you; that ye, always having all sufficiency in all things, may abound to every good work: [9] (As is written, He had dispersed abroad; he had given to the poor: his righteousness remaineth for ever.**

*[In the next verse, you'll see that you don't have to worry about where the seed is going to come from. You will only need a heart of grace to recognize the season.]*

**[10] Now, he that ministereth seed to the sower both minister bread for your food while you're sowing and multiply your seed sown and increase the fruit of your righteousness;**

2 Corinthians 9:8-10

Say to the Lord, "Teach me how to maximize

my sowing." With that request, you are asking the Lord to maximize your harvest, to maximize your financial life, and to maximize your right out of the world's system. The word "maximize" means to make something as large or as great as possible. You don't have to depend on the world's system anymore.

---

**SAY THIS ALOUD**

*Lord, teach me how to maximize my sowing. Teach me how to make my seeds as large or as great as possible. Let me make the best use of my seed. I want to maximize it. Let me make the best use of this seed privilege you have given me. I am ready to sow myself off of the world's system.*

Cast down imaginations that are blocking the flow of God's prosperity in your life.

DR. LEROY THOMPSON SR.

# 8.

# Catch The Seed Blocker

In the night watch, at about three o'clock in the morning, I saw myself dealing with what seemed like a small monster. In the dream, I would run and look for him, and when I would find and grab him, he'd somehow get away from me. I kept running, and he kept getting away from me. That's how it was for a while, and then, the scene changed. All of a sudden, I was in a different setting, teaching on the principles of how to get out of debt and how to get set free. As I'm standing there teaching, I see a really short man in the service wearing a brown suit. He wasn't sitting in a chair like the congregation. He was on the floor, lying on a pillow — just looking at me, watching me teach. He was comfortable, and I could tell he had been there for a long time. He had obviously created a homestead there.

For a while, he stayed still, calmly lying on his

pillow, until I got to a point in my teaching about sowing effectively. When he heard this, he jumped up and ran toward me. When I saw him coming, I took my left foot and popped him in the chest. I hit him multiple times.

At that exact moment, my wife yelled out, "What are you doing?" I had kicked her pretty hard in my sleep. She didn't know I wasn't kicking *her*; I was dealing with that man in my dream.

Now, *who* was that? Who was that little short man? The Holy Ghost revealed to me in the night watch that it was a seed-blocking demon who had *been* in the Church and had gotten comfortable. Everyone else was in chairs, but he had been there so long that he'd stretched out on a pillow. He'd been there for centuries, waiting to start blocking when he hears someone teaching about finances. That night, I took his demonic power off of the Church.

The Church has suffered long enough because of a rank of seed-blocking demons standing in the way. There are fallen angels whose only job is to block you from the revelation of sowing and from being a bonafide sower. There are harvest-blocking demons, too. If they can't block the seed, they try to block the harvest. Knowing this also led me to the conclusion that there must be tithe-blocking demons as well.

With authority, I have apostolically dealt with them all. They're gone from the Church. Make sure they're gone from your house and gone from out of your life! They can't block your harvest anymore. They can't block your prosperity. They can't block your wealth. They can't block your breakthrough, your joy, or your comfort. They can't block your increase.

From this day forward, don't allow your needs to block your seed, either. Most times, that's fear trying to keep you from sowing, but it has no business holding your financial freedom back. Instead of letting your need for something block your seed, let your *seed* block your need. That little demon has been lying down there, blocking you from sowing — but we've caught him.

Anytime you catch a demon, a territory is cleared. Therefore, there has been a path cleared for you to go to a place of no limits in your life. You are not in the same position you were in when you first opened this book. With this realization and freedom, you can have what your heart desires, right now. You were born and designed to take over, and the enemy knows it.

The enemy may have been trying to block your seed, but no more can he stop you. We caught him in the spirit. With that seed-blocking demon out of the way and your faith aligned, your money can flow as it should.

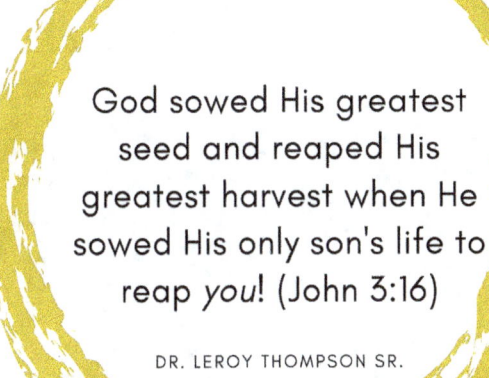

God sowed His greatest seed and reaped His greatest harvest when He sowed His only son's life to reap *you*! (John 3:16)

DR. LEROY THOMPSON SR.

# 9.
# Take the Weights Off

**Wherefore seeing we also are compassed about with so great a cloud of witnesses, <u>let us lay aside every weight</u>, and the sin which doth so easily beset us, and let us run with patience the race that is set before us,**

**Hebrews 12:1**

The Church has not fully understood "sowing faith." I think there's been a trembling happening around this sowing faith because people are attached to their money and are questioning the process when they give. The five weights that can be on someone's seeds are the following: *when, how, who, where,* and *what.*

*When is it going to happen?* They ask. *How is it going to happen? Who is God going to use? Where will they come from? Why it hasn't come yet?*

If you are asking these questions, you have to stop and finally turn your seed loose! Lay aside those weights on your seed, and let God do His part. God determines *who* he's going to use in the process of bringing your harvest to you. God determines *how* it's going to all work out. Remember, the blocking demon has been taken off of your seed, but now you must take the weight off your seed.

Your job is to look beyond present situations and forget about those five weights. I want you to see yourself out of debt. See yourself driving the best. See yourself wearing the best. See yourself living with the best of everything.

Jesus sowed himself as a seed so that you can be rich. *You* are the rich harvest of Jesus the Seed. The greatest prosperity you have is that you belong to God.

God isn't concerned with silver or gold and all that stuff. I mean, the streets in heaven are paved with gold. Doesn't that tell us something? If a man talked about taking his gold with him to heaven, God would say, "Look at that highway down here. In heaven, we walk on that. The only thing that amounts to anything precious in heaven is you."

You are so precious to God; you are *His* prosperity. You can be confident that He'll always go above and beyond to take care of you. Take those weights off your seed, and trust the process that God has set up to bless you with more than enough in this world.

> **SAY THIS ALOUD**
>
> *I'm God's prosperity.*

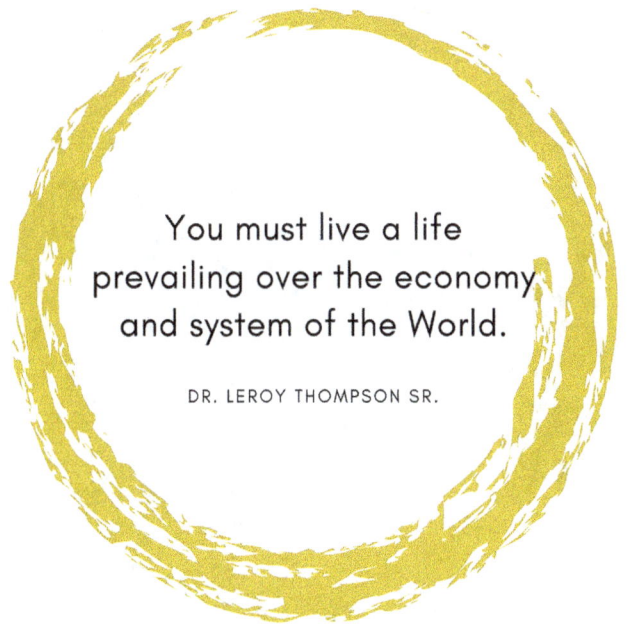

You must live a life
prevailing over the economy
and system of the World.

DR. LEROY THOMPSON SR.

# 10.

# The Seed Always Prevails

"Yes indeed, it won't be long now." God's Decree. "<u>Things are going to happen so fast your head will swim, one thing fast on the heels of the other. You won't be able to keep up</u>. Everything will be happening at once—and everywhere you look, blessings! Blessings like wine pouring off the mountains and hills. I'll make everything right again for my people Israel:

*They'll rebuild their ruined cities.*
*They'll plant vineyards and drink good wine.*
*They'll work their gardens and eat fresh vegetables.*
*And I'll plant them, plant them on their own land.*
*They'll never again be uprooted from the land I've given them."*

> **God, your God, says so.**
>
> **Amos 9:13-15 (MSG)**

The seed is designed by God to prevail. When it's wrapped in faith, it happens just as you see it recorded in Amos 9. Once you sow in faith, **it won't be long. Things are going to happen so fast your head will swim. One thing quickly on the heels of the other.** In other words, when the blessings start flowing, you always have more coming in. It just keeps on coming. That's the way it happened to me.

When you leave broke, as a location, you leave it forever. I left broke years ago. It took me a long time to leave it, but I left it. And I know I'll never go back to broke again. Once you go on to function in the revelation, reality, and redemptive forces of leaving broke, you never go back! That's why the Lord gave me the prophetic word, *I'll never be broke another day in my life*. I can't even think broke. I can't even go to any broke content in my mind. God wiped it out. He eradicated it because I know the system of God. And I know it's real.

There's a place called *Believing* and there's a

place called *Knowing*. Any revelation that you step into far enough, you come to a point where you're no longer *believing* it — you *know* it. That's where I am. I'm in Knowing, and if you hold on to this revelation, you can be there, too.

I'm a blessed man. It didn't happen by accident or because I'm someone special. It happened because I followed God close enough to hear what He was saying, and I did what He told me to do. Consistently sowing pulled down all the financial giants in my life and money started coming in from everywhere.

When we read the parable in Matthew 13:1-11, we have to wonder why Jesus would teach about the sower who sows the seed. It reads:

**[1] The same day went Jesus out of the house, and sat by the sea side. [2] And great multitudes were gathered together unto him, so that he went into a ship, and sat; and the whole multitude stood on the shore.**

**[3] And he spake many things unto them in parables, saying, Behold, a sower went forth to sow; [4] And when he sowed, some seeds fell by the way side, and the fowls came and devoured**

**them up: [5] Some fell upon stony places, where they had not much earth: and forthwith they sprung up, because they had no deepness of earth: [6] And when the sun was up, they were scorched; and because they had no root, they withered away. [7] And some fell among thorns; and the thorns sprung up, and choked them: [8] But other fell into good ground, and brought forth fruit, some an hundredfold, some sixtyfold, some thirtyfold. [9] Who hath ears to hear, let him hear.**

**[10] And the disciples came, and said unto him, Why speakest thou unto them in parables? [11] He answered and said unto them, Because it is given unto you to know the mysteries of the kingdom of heaven, but to them it is not given.**

**Matthew 13:1-11**

Throughout the parable, Jesus is talking about different types of soil and different types of outcomes. After he answers the disciples in verse 11 saying, *Because it's given to you to know the mystery of the kingdom of heaven, but to them it's not given,* He goes on to verse 12 to say: **For whoso-**

**ever has, to him shall be given, and he shall have more abundance: but whosoever has not, from him shall be taken away even that he has**. I believe the seed instruction is here. Sowing is a mystery of the kingdom of heaven, and it brings mysterious results. All seeds have the audacity to produce a harvest, but Jesus is saying, "If you don't have that revelation, whatever you do have will be taken from you. But, if you have the revelation right, whatever you have, you're going to have more abundant."

From verses 11 and 12, Jesus reveals that sowing is a kingdom purpose that cannot be denied. In other words, "seed sowing" is not all about you. It is about the kingdom. It's about representing God. I believe prosperity is a high calling that we *must* continue to push toward.

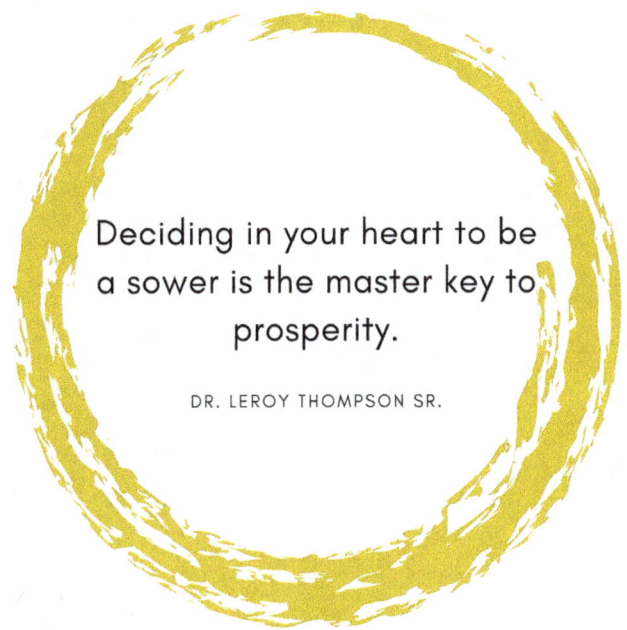

Deciding in your heart to be a sower is the master key to prosperity.

DR. LEROY THOMPSON SR.

## 11.

# Be a Seed Pusher

> **I <u>press toward the mark for the prize of the high calling</u> of God in Christ Jesus.**
> **Philippians 3:14**

When people or demons try to stop you from giving, you will have to press to sow — press to do what God told you to do. You have to press for the mark of being the sower that God called you to be.

The enemy doesn't want you to pass the sowing test. He knows that once you've passed it, you will graduate to another level. The good news is that not only does God give you the test but He also gives you the answer, the seed, the grace, the courage and the confidence to pass it! God has this set up to take you out of this earthly financial rat race.

May God give you a seed-pusher anointing. When your natural mind tells you, *You can't do that. You will never go there.* This anointing will help you push past it, sow, and go anyway. You know how there are drug pushers in the world? Well, it's time we push something. I know there are some seed pushers reading this now.

You must never become comfortable with just enough. *Push.* God will give you the seed, the soil, and the harvest. *Keep pushing.* Your part is to consistently prepare and plan to sow ahead of time. You have to purposely put yourself in that position, because if not, God won't just give it to you.

In First Kings 17, the prophet Elijah came across the widow woman and told her to "make me a cake". She had planned for her and her child to eat the handful of meal she had left in a barrel and a little oil in a cruse and then wait to die. Elijah knew otherwise. He said to her, "Fear not. You don't understand what I'm sent here for. I'm sent here to put you in another category. You're not going to die. The Lord said to me, the barrel of meal shall not waste, neither shall the cruse of oil fail. But, you have to make me a cake, first."

She made the cake and the meal kept rising in the barrel. In verses 15-16 of that same chapter, it states: **And she went and did according to the saying of Elijah: and she, and he, and her house, did eat many days. And the barrel of meal wasted not, neither did the cruse of oil fail, according to the word of the Lord, which he spake by Elijah.**

I see the meal rising in your life. Notice, that meal didn't rise from the top — it kept coming up from the bottom. Nobody could explain it, but God's hand was under that barrel bringing it up. I see God's hand under your finances, too. When God's hand gets under your finances, you'll start rising up. No one will be able to stop it, and you won't be able to explain it.

Zechariah 8:12 says: **For the seed shall be prosperous; the vine shall give her fruit, and the ground shall give her increase, and the heavens shall give their dew; and I will cause the remnant of this people to possess all these things.** Give the seed time to prosper, and it will.

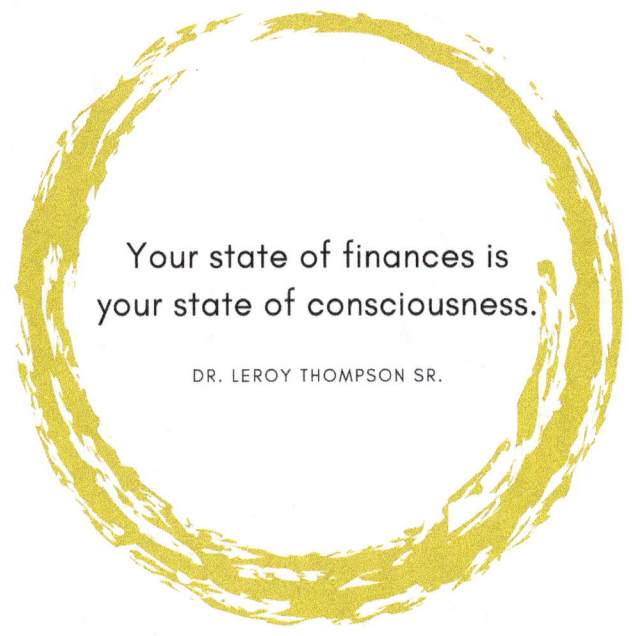

Your state of finances is your state of consciousness.

DR. LEROY THOMPSON SR.

## 12.

## Be Adventurous

I'm so glad Carolyn and I went through all of the things we did to get here. I remember when the Lord told her, "Build a big house. I'll show it to you." At the time, we were as broke as a skunk on a log in the water. Let me show you how God works. My wife saw the house in a vision, and then God sent a Baptist deacon who knew nothing about prosperity to tell us that he saw us living in a big house with lots of lights around it.

Remember, we didn't have any money, but when two of our church members told us about a builder in New Orleans we should visit, we went! We were sitting in his office lobby area, waiting for him to meet with us, when we looked up and saw a picture of the house my wife envisioned on the wall. When the builder came out of his office to introduce himself, we told him in confidence that we were interested in *that* kind of house, the one in the picture on the wall. The builder went on to tell us that it was actually a photo of his house, and then, he offered to take us to see it.

Fast forward sometime later, I sit down with my banker to see about getting what was needed to build.

"Mr. Thompson, you're a pastor," he says. "Why do you want a house like that?"

"Why do you have a house like you do?" I'm quick to reply. "You live just down the street from where I wanna build. Y'all don't tell me what to build. I'm gonna build it!"

I went to four or five more banks, and they all turned me down. I just kept going anyway. Until finally, I landed a bank that let me have it. Fast forward again, and you'll see we paid them back for a thirty-year mortgage in three years! God can do these kinds of things for you, too. Are you hearing me?

Let me show you another way God works. You may have heard the story of when I quit my job because God told me to. Well, again, we didn't have much money, but my wife was still working. One day, I went to pick up her paycheck, and before I could make it to the bank to cash it, I lost it. Soon after, a woman called my wife's job, and asked for her.

"Are you Carolyn Thompson?" she asked.

"Yeah, I'm Carolyn Thompson," my wife replied.

"*I'm* Carolyn Thompson," the woman on the other end of the phone said. "And I just found your check."

Shockingly, the name of the woman who found the check was Carolyn Thompson, too. She could have easily cashed it and never called. I believe this was the Lord telling Carolyn and me, "You're going in the right direction, and I can take care of you no matter what happens." Today, I can go on and on with situations like this of God stepping in and providing for us.

You have to be adventurous in the spirit. You have to know that in some areas you're going to be a pioneer, and you won't have any tracks to follow. Every now and then, you're going to have to make some *fresh* tracks, especially to help those coming behind you. For example, I didn't qualify in the natural realm, so when people turned me down, I had to make fresh tracks. Now, those tracks are helping you! That's what God's looking for — someone to make fresh tracks.

Sure, people will try to tell you that you can't go into better-off areas in life, but you *can* go there. It may take time, but you'll get there. You may have tried to do something, and it didn't work, but that doesn't mean that you can't have it. Keep looking unto Jesus, and you will end up in the right scene (Heb. 12.2).

Don't set the trials before you; set the joy before you. Again, be adventurous! On the other side of the tests and trials, there's a seat waiting on you. When you know this, the enemy can't pull any more tricks on you. He can't hold up your harvest or abundance. If one person turns you down, go to another one. Go until you get the answer you want. You don't have to depend on *them*. Depend on *Him*.

They may talk to you any kind of way, but make sure you stay on the line with the Father. Keep operating in faith, and you can't be turned down. You are the Father's child. Everything belongs to Him; therefore, everything belongs to *you*. God wants you to have the best, and when you're adventurous in faith, no one in this world can keep you from that.

Your harvest is in your spirit. It's your soul that has to be dealt with.

DR. LEROY THOMPSON SR.

## 13.

# Manifest From Within

To manifest financial freedom in your life, you *must* deal with financial imprisonment from within.

Your financial condition is not based on your wallet, purse, checking account, race, level of education, paycheck, or political stance — it's based on whether you have a trained or untrained soul. As I briefly covered in Chapter 6, the soul includes your mind, consciousness, imagination, will, reasoning, desires, and emotions. It is designed to correlate with your spirit, but your spirit won't manifest as it should if your soul is not in order.

You can pray in the spirit and activate the divinity that's within you but then never see it as a reality in your life. Why is that? It's because your spirit has to come *through* your soul to manifest from within, and when your soul is not properly aligned, your spirit fails. For example, let's say you've been consistent with affirmations, confessions, decrees and scripture readings on wealth, prosperity, and abundance, but you stop there. If that's the case, everything you're doing is insufficient, because unless you align your soul with your spirit, you'll never see those affirmations, confessions, decrees, and scriptures manifest in your physical life.

The spirit, soul, and body *must* connect to produce. However, for years, the Church has suffered financially by not understanding this alignment of the spirit, soul, and body and by not knowing that the *total* man has to be intact in order to have manifestation and demonstration. Take a look at Hebrews 4:12.

**For the word of God is quick, and powerful, and sharper than any two-edged sword, piercing even to <u>the dividing asunder of soul and spirit</u>, and of the joints and marrow, and is a discerner of <u>the thoughts and intents of the heart</u>.**

**Hebrews 4:12**

The thoughts and intents of the soul can only be rightly divided and aligned by the Word of God

— not just by good teaching or preaching. The individual who is being ministered to must actually be open to the fact that God is trying to say something to him or her in their *mind*. Once their mind is aligned, this person will see manifestations.

Now, let's read Romans 12:1-3. These verses are directly connected to Hebrews 4:12.

**[1] I beseech you therefore, brethren, by the mercies of God, that ye present your bodies a living sacrifice, holy, acceptable unto God, which is your reasonable service. [2] And <u>be not conformed to this world: but be ye transformed by the renewing of your mind</u>, that ye may prove what is that good, and acceptable, and perfect, will of God. [3] For I say, through the grace given unto me, to every man that is among you, not to think of himself more highly than he ought to think; but to think soberly, according as God hath dealt to every man the measure of faith.**

**Romans 12:1-3**

In Romans 12:2, it says **be not conformed** but **be transformed by the renewing of your mind**.

What do you think it means to renew your mind? It means to properly run your soul — to properly run your consciousness, will, reasoning, desires, and emotions — and to properly run your supernatural camera called the imagination.

When it comes to running the soul, most of the Body of Christ is in an incubator stage. They can't manifest the divinity within on the outside because their spirits are overwhelmed by the persecution of the enemy through their minds. In Psalm 142:3, David says: **When my <u>spirit was overwhelmed within me</u>, then thou knewest my path. In the way wherein I walked have they privily laid a snare for me**. When he said "my spirit was overwhelmed," what do you think he meant? What do you think causes a believer's spirit to be overwhelmed? You'll see it again in Psalm 143:3-4. It reads:

**[3] <u>For the enemy hath persecuted my soul</u>; he hath smitten my life down to the ground; he hath made me to dwell in darkness, as those that have been long dead. [4] <u>Therefore is my spirit overwhelmed within me</u>; my heart within me is desolate.**

### Psalm 143:4

In verse three, David says why his spirit was overwhelmed within him in verse four: **For the enemy hath persecuted my soul—**. Notice, the enemy attacks the soul — the mind, consciousness, emotions, imagination, will, and desire. This type of attack overwhelms, or blocks, your spirit and keeps it from manifesting the blessings of God in your life as it should. For this reason, you must continuously focus and operate on your soul to break free of financial imprisonment from within.

This operation takes the enemy out of the way and allows your spirit and soul to connect. When that connection happens on the inside, the flow of financial blessings will start producing floods on the outside that you will not be able to keep up with.

God deals with your spirit, but *you* have to deal with your soul. As you get your mind in alignment with the Word of God, the manifestation and demonstration will hit your finances. It'll open up what is already within you. You see, the harvest has already been sent. It's in you right now. You've been walking around packing the harvest this entire time. God has not held that back from you. Your harvest was deposited in your spirit as soon as you paid your tithe and sowed your seed. You see, you have so much money in you! It's time to unlock it, unblock it, and unstop it.

Now, when the operation begins in your soul, two things will happen: John 6:63 and Romans 8:2.

**It is the spirit that quickeneth; the flesh profiteth nothing: the words that I speak unto you, they are spirit, and they are life.**

**John 6:63**

**For the law of the Spirit of life in Christ Jesus hath made me free from the law of sin and death.**

**Romans 8:2**

When the operation in your soul begins, you will stir up the spirit and life that's within you, and you will be free by the law of the Spirit of life in Christ Jesus that no man or demon can stand up to. Let's take it further and read Ephesians 3:14-20. Apostle Paul was performing surgery in the soul with these scriptures.

**[14] For this cause I bow my knees unto the**

**Father of our Lord Jesus Christ, [15] Of whom the whole family in heaven and earth is named, [16] That he would grant you, according to the riches of his glory, to be strengthened with might by his Spirit in the inner man; [17] That Christ may dwell in your hearts by faith; that ye, being rooted and grounded in love, [18] May be able to comprehend with all saints what is the breadth, and length, and depth, and height; [19] And to know the love of Christ, which passeth knowledge, that ye might be filled with all the fulness of God.** (*May you be filled in your soul, too!*)

**[20] Now unto him that is able to do exceeding abundantly above all that we ask or think, according to the power that worketh in us**
**Ephesians 3:14-20**

In verse 20, Paul says: **Now unto him that is able to do exceeding abundantly above all that we ask or think.** That's how it should be in your life. You don't want to live normally, do you? You're about to see **exceeding abundantly above all that you ask or think** in your life. You are about to excel in every way. You haven't arrived at your rightful place until you can say, "I don't know how much I have. I'm tired of counting!" That's God's best for you — a life of financial freedom and manifestation.

You are getting your soul out of prison at this very moment and becoming free to sow and grow rich as you should. Coming out of financial imprisonment in your mind, will, desire, imagination and emotions will cause divine manifestations of abundance to follow. Remember, God has already sent your harvest. It has always been in you; except now, you know how to unblock your soul and freely receive it through God's financial plan for you called sowing.

As the Father works with you, follow what He tells you to do without second guessing it. The process of sowing and growing rich is not a crowd deal. It's personal. Everyone has to go to the table for themselves. It cannot be done on an escalator, nor on an elevator. You have to take the stairs. Every step you take in sowing from this moment forward will prepare you for your next level in growing rich.

> **SAY THIS ALOUD**
>
> *I'm going to let the Holy Ghost operate on my finances, starting with my soul, right now.*

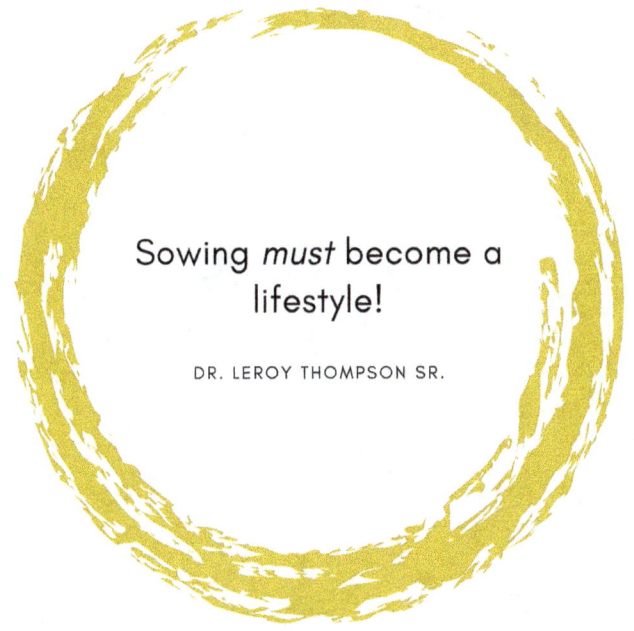

Sowing *must* become a lifestyle!

DR. LEROY THOMPSON SR.

## Keep this in your heart.

Here are three statements to keep in your heart and meditate on:

- Sowing is a blessing from God to make you rich.
- "Holy Spirit, develop a pure desire in me to sow."
- Sowing destroys all financial impossibilities.

If you meditate on these three statements, your life will begin to change almost instantly. Remember, the kingdom of God is a seed kingdom. Therefore, sow like you own money, and don't let money own *you*.

> **SAY THIS ALOUD**
>
> *God has a supernatural financial plan for me called sowing!*

## About the Author

Louisiana native, Dr. (Apostle) Leroy Thompson Sr. is the Pastor of Word of Life Christian Center and Chief overseer of Leroy Thompson Ministerial Association (LTMA) and Ever Increasing Word Ministries.

With a strong calling from God, Apostle Thompson travels the world taking the message of financial freedom to the Body of Christ by holding *Money Cometh to You Conferences*. He truly believes that God's financial abundance is for every believer. He is the author of several books, including his bestseller "Money Cometh! To The Body of Christ."

Apostle Thompson not only believes but also knows from experience that the key to a successful ministry is the combination of praying in the spirit, living and teaching the Word of Faith, and following after the leadership of the Holy Ghost.

He has been happily married to his lovely wife,

Mrs. Carolyn A. Thompson, for over 40 years. They have four children — Leroy Jr. (Shantel), Shauna (Jesse), Donavan, and Darnell (Deirdre) — who serve full-time in the ministry along with their parents.

## About the Publisher

Ever Increasing Word Ministries (EIWM) is the outreach ministry of Word of Life Christian Center. The vision of EIWM is "Changing the Lives of People with the Word of God" and "Equipping the Body of Christ to Evangelize the World." Thousands of partners from around the world help us to achieve this purpose. If you would like to know more about EIWM, visit eiwm.org.

**Ever Increasing Word Ministries**
P.O. Box 7
Darrow, LA 70725

# Become a Financial Freedom Partner

What does it mean to become a partner? It means you are in agreement with this vision and this vision is in agreement with you in your finances!

**Proverbs 29:18 states:**

**Where there is no vision, the people perish: but he that keepeth the law, happy is he.**

Partnership privileges include the following:

- Regular prayer from this ministry for your success and victory

- A Monthly impartation and update letter from us.

- A Monthly CD or MP3 teaching from Apostle Thompson.

- An Official Financial Freedom Membership Card that enables you to a 20% discount on any products ordered from this ministry.

- **Support who #WeSupport**
    - Mercy Ships
    - Christ For All Nations
    - Jewish Voice Ministries International
    - Samaritan's Purse
- **Most importantly, exercising the impartation and information you receive to produce the God-fulfilled life!**

To sign up and learn more about becoming a partner with EIWM, please visit eiwm.org/partnership.

## Connect to LeroyThompson.TV

By visiting **leroythompson.tv**, you receive 24/7, free access to the archives of all services and conferences held by Dr. Leroy Thompson Sr. Here, you can also watch LIVE broadcasts from Dr. Thompson's *Sunday Worship* services at 9 AM CST, *Training in the Word* services held every Tuesday at 7 PM CST, as well as all *Money Cometh To You Conferences* held around the country throughout the year.

Have access to Roku? Add the EIWM channel for on-demand video access.

## Stay tuned and stay connected!

# Other Books by Dr. Leroy Thompson Sr.

- ***Looking in the Mirror:*** *Know Who You Are*
- ***Never Go After Money:*** *And Money Will Come After You*
- ***Beyond Breakthrough:*** *His Church, Your Keys*
- ***Cross Factor:*** *The Inherent Benefits of the Blood*
- *No More Empty Hands*
- *5 Ways to Failure Proof Your Giving*
- *Becoming a Commander of Covenant Wealth*
- *You're Not Broke You Have a Seed*
- *I'll Never Be Broke Another Day in My Life*

- ***Framing Your World with the Word of God***
- ***Money With a Mission***
- ***Dynamic Laws of Money Cometh***
- ***Money Thou Art Loosed***
- ***What To Do When Your Faith is Challenged***
- ***How to Find Your Wealthy Place***
- ***The Voice of Jesus:*** *Speaking God's Word with Authority*
- ***Money Cometh!*** *To The Body of Christ*

If this book has been a blessing to you or if you would like to see more of the Ever Increasing Word Ministries' product line, please visit the EIWM online store at www.eiwm.org/estore.

www.ingramcontent.com/pod-product-compliance
Lightning Source LLC
Chambersburg PA
CBHW050601300426

44112CB00013B/2023